This book belongs to

This is a Dressy Countess Book
First Published in 2016

www.dressycountess.com

All rights reserved. No part of this publication maybe reproduced, stored in a retrieval system, or transmitted in any form or by any means, electronic, mechanical, photocopying, recording or otherwise, without the prior consent of the copyright owner(Dressy Countess).

ISBN 978-0-9948772-0-8

Printed in U.S.A.

That's All Me.

Written by Mia D.

Illustrated by Dressy Countess

Kiddykido woke up on her face.
Seeing her room out of it's place.Who messed up
my neat room? Puppy, it wasn't you I assume.
Maybe another kid?! with a cute costume?!

Then she started to
search everywhere, behind the sofa,
upon floors, search the halls,
Behind the walls, inside of the bathroom
of each room.
The wardrobe, between towels.
Maybe she is in little jars. She searched, searched
and searched. She really did search hard that day.

Maybe she was so small,
like a little fireball. Hiding in the cabinets!
Go to the kitchen...,
Go to the kitchen...
Checked inside of the tea cups..
In the freezer, behind the ice cream bars..
Would that be far!

She even looked inside
of the toilet. Lifted up the lid,
had a quick peek, had a blush on her cheek
No one was there!

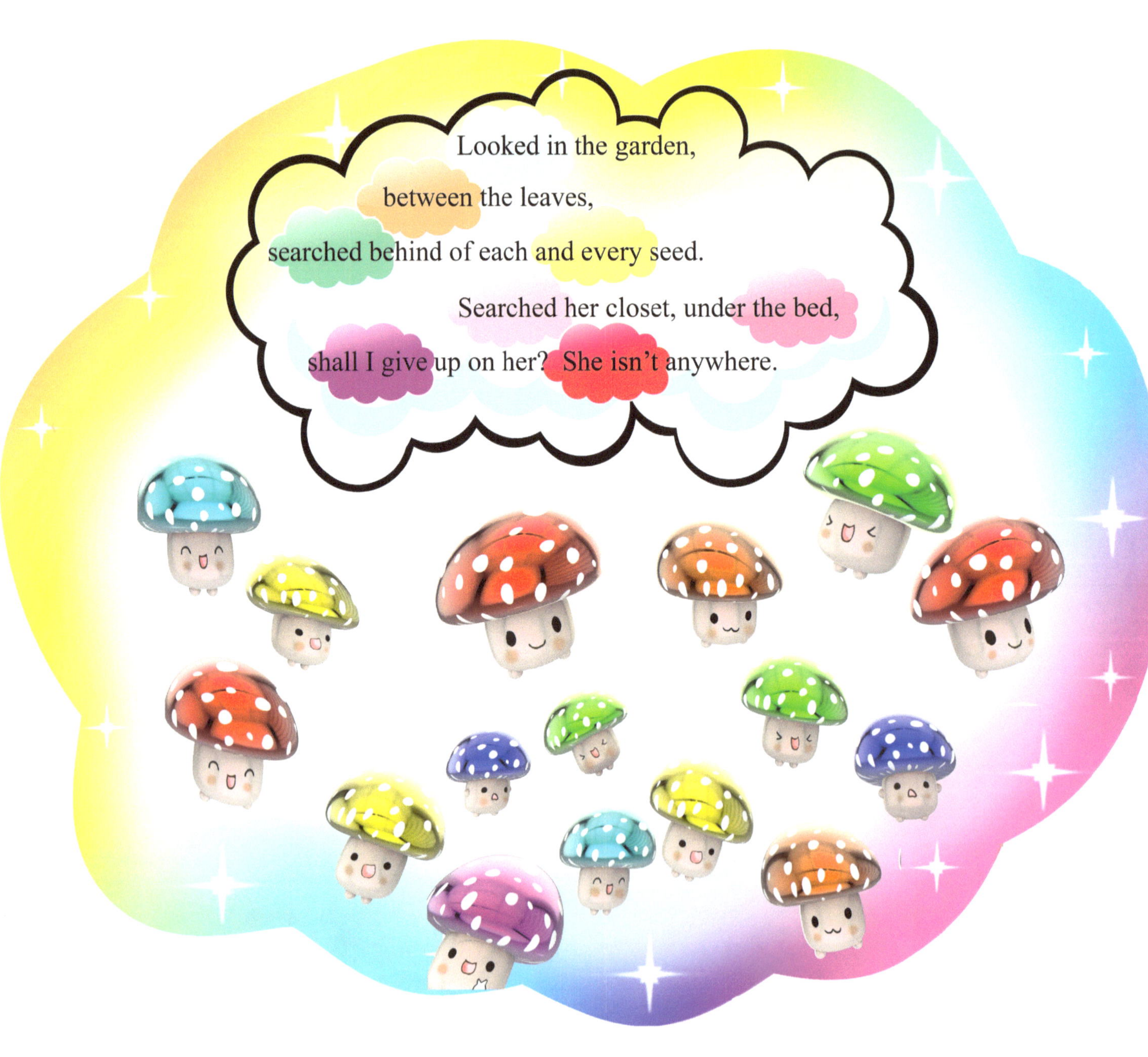
Looked in the garden,
between the leaves,
searched behind of each and every seed.
Searched her closet, under the bed,
shall I give up on her? She isn't anywhere.

Then I decided to go far.
Got into my daddy's car...Daddy looked in his rear mirror.
He said: "Did you close your seatbelt?"
I was so sad, so upset. Didn't wanna listen a bit.
I said "Daisy, Daisy I feel so lazy."
LUNA

"There she is", Daddy said.
"I can see her, that is her"! I looked at the mirror.
No one was there, was only me. She wasn't there...
Then daddy said: "Look again!
That is Kiddykido, but not the same..."

I looked again, so confused.
Saw her right by my sight.
The tongue was out, the eyes were shot
Could it be her? Daddy said: “That is her!
Whom you were looking for,
every minute of today...” Kiddykido said:
“I am Kiddykido, who are you?”
Why did you mess up my house?

"My name is Coontassi"
The girl in the mirror said.
"Love to do, fun to do, that's all I want to do"
"With giggle like pig, I go arround, do dig"
Some words stays on my head.
But some things won't stick.
I have my very own talents.
Like no one else you know.
Sometime I like to let them show.
I can do great things.
I can do many don'ts ....BUT
Not always get a kiss at the end!

I want to learn and know things,
trying many games, but not always so smart.
Sometimes I do little farts. Maybe I could get
clever! Sometimes it seems it takes forever.
Maybe I should have a seat,
read some books that are neat. Haven't
done that for awhile. A book with lots of pics.
With big letters of A and B's.
So maybe you should the same
Please read my next book
I let you know the fun things
That's how Coontassi tales begins...

E=MC2
Energy = Milk Cookie (Two)!

Things Coontassi told me to do, but I am not going to!

Find Us @
www.dressycountess.com

www.ingramcontent.com/pod-product-compliance
Lightning Source LLC
Chambersburg PA
CBHW042140030726
47599CB00002B/551
* 9 7 8 0 9 9 4 8 7 7 2 0 8 *